ZEN

POEMS & SAYINGS

ZEN
POEMS & SAYINGS

ISBN: 1 86476 360 4

AXIOM
AUSTRALIA

www.axiompublishers.com.au

Printed in Malaysia

I live far off in the wild
Where moss and woods are thick and plants perfumed.
I can see mountains rain or shine
And never hear market noise.
I light a few leaves in my stove to heat tea.
To patch my robe I cut off a cloud.
Lifetimes seldom fill a hundred years.
Why suffer for profit and fame?

In autumn
even though I may
see it again,
how can I sleep
with the moon this evening?

— *Dogen*

New Year's first snow—ah—
just barely enough to tilt
the daffodil.

— *Basho*

Faith In Mind

The Supreme Way is not difficult
If only you do not pick and choose.
Neither love nor hate,
And you will clearly understand.
Be off by a hair,
And you are as far apart as heaven from earth.
If you want it to appear,
Be neither for nor against.
For and against opposing each other—
This is the mind's disease.
Without recognising the mysterious principle
It is useless to practice quietude.

The Way is perfect like great space,
Without lack, without excess.
Because of grasping and rejecting,
You cannot attain it.
Do not pursue conditioned existence;
Do not abide in acceptance of emptiness.
In oneness and equality,
Confusion vanishes of itself.
Stop activity and return to stillness,
And that stillness will be even more active.
Only stagnating in duality,
How can you recognise oneness?

If you fail to penetrate oneness,
Both places lose their function.
Banish existence and you fall into existence;
Follow emptiness and you turn your back on it.
Excessive talking and thinking
Turn you from harmony with the Way.
Cut off talking and thinking,
And there is nowhere you cannot penetrate.
Return to the root and attain the principle;
Pursue illumination and you lose it.
One moment of reversing the light
Is greater than the previous emptiness.
The previous emptiness is transformed;
It was all a product of deluded views.
No need to seek the real;
Just extinguish your views.

Do not abide in dualistic views;
take care not to seek after them.
As soon as there is right and wrong
The mind is scattered and lost.
Two comes from one,
Yet do not even keep the one.
When one mind does not arise,
Myriad dharmas are without defect.
Without defect, without dharmas,
No arising, no mind.

The subject is extinguished with the object.
The object sinks away with the subject.
Object is object because of the subject;
Subject is subject because of the object.
Know that the two
Are originally one emptiness.
In one emptiness the two are the same,
Containing all phenomena.
Not seeing fine or coarse,
How can there be any bias?

The Great Way is broad,
Neither easy nor difficult.
With narrow views and doubts,
Haste will slow you down.
Attach to it and you lose the measure;
The mind will enter a deviant path.
Let it go and be spontaneous,
Experience no going or staying.

Accord with your nature, unite with the Way,
Wander at ease, without vexation.
Bound by thoughts, you depart from the real;
And sinking into a stupor is as bad.
It is not good to weary the spirit.
Why alternate between aversion and affection?

If you wish to enter the one vehicle,
Do not be repelled by the sense realm.
With no aversion to the sense realm,
You become one with true enlightenment.
The wise have no motives;
Fools put themselves in bondage.
One dharma is not different from another.
The deluded mind clings to whatever it desires.
Using mind to cultivate mind—
Is this not a great mistake?

The erring mind begets tranquillity and confusion;
In enlightenment there are no likes or dislikes.
The duality of all things
Issues from false discriminations.
A dream, an illusion, a flower in the sky—
How could they be worth grasping?
Gain and loss, right and wrong—
Discard them all at once.

If the eyes do not close in sleep,
All dreams will cease of themselves.
If the mind does not discriminate,
All dharmas are of one suchness.
The essence of one suchness is profound;
Unmoving, conditioned things are forgotten.
Contemplate all dharmas as equal,

And you return to things as they are.
When the subject disappears,
There can be no measuring or comparing.

Stop activity and there is no activity;
When activity stops, there is no rest.
Since two cannot be established,
How can there be one?
In the very ultimate,
Rules and standards do not exist.

Develop a mind of equanimity,
And all deeds are put to rest.
Anxious doubts are completely cleared.
Right faith is made upright.
Nothing lingers behind,
Nothing can be remembered.
Bright and empty, functioning naturally,
The mind does not exert itself.
It is not a place of thinking,
Difficult for reason and emotion to fathom.
In the Dharma Realm of true suchness,
There is no other, no self.

To accord with it is vitally important;
Only refer to "not-two."
In not-two all things are in unity;

Nothing is not included.
The wise throughout the ten directions
All enter this principle.
This principle is neither hurried nor slow—
One thought for ten thousand years.

Abiding nowhere yet everywhere,
The ten directions are right before you.
The smallest is the same as the largest
In the realm where delusion is cut off.
The largest is the same as the smallest;
No boundaries are visible.
Existence is precisely emptiness;
Emptiness is precisely existence.
If it is not like this,
Then you must not preserve it.

One is everything;
Everything is one.
If you can be like this,
Why worry about not finishing?
Faith and mind are not two;
Non-duality is faith in mind.

The path of words is cut off;
There is no past, no future, no present.

— *Seng Ts'an,*

Be equal to every hindrance. Buddha attained.
Supreme Enlightenment without hindrance.
Seekers after truth are schooled in adversity.
When they are confronted by a hindrance, they can't be
over-come. Then, cutting free, their treasure is great.

This body's existence is like a bubble's
may as well accept what happens
events and hopes seldom agree
but who can step back doesn't worry
we blossom and fade like flowers
gather and part like clouds
worldly thoughts I forgot long ago
relaxing all day on a peak.

Do not permit the events of your daily life
    to bind you,
but never withdraw yourself from them.

One day while walking through the wilderness a man stumbled upon a vicious tiger. He ran but soon came to the edge of a high cliff. Desperate to save himself, he climbed down a vine and dangled over the fatal precipice. As he hung there, two mice appeared from a hole in the cliff and began gnawing on the vine. Suddenly, he noticed on the vine a plump wild strawberry. He plucked it and popped it in his mouth. It was incredibly delicious!

My Ch'an hut leans at the summit
Clouds sail back and forth
A waterfall hangs in front
A mountain ridge crests in back
On a rock wall I sketched three buddhas
For incense there's plum branch in a jar
The fields below might be level
But can't match a mountain home free of dust.

I searched creation without success
Then by chance found this forested ridge
My thatch hut cuts through heaven's blue
A moss-slick trail through dense bamboo
Others are moved by profit and fame
I grow old living for Ch'an
Pine trees and strange rocks remain unknown
To those who look for mind with mind.

You're bound to become a buddha if you practice
If water drips long enough even rocks wear through
It's not true thick skulls can't be pierced
People just imagine their minds are hard.

Summer grasses:
all that remains of great soldiers'
imperial dreams.

— *Basho*

Standing outside my pointed-roof hut
Who'd guess how spacious it is inside
A galaxy of worlds is there
With room to spare for a zazen cushion.

Becoming a buddha is easy
But ending illusions is hard
So many frosted moonlit nights
I've sat and felt
The cold before dawn.

On the white poppy,
a butterfly's torn wing
is a keepsake.

— Basho

If all the waves of the Zen stream were alike,
innumerable ordinary people would get bogged down.

An old grave hidden away at the foot of a deserted
 hill,
Overrun with rank weeks growing unchecked year after
 year;
There is no one left to tend the tomb,
And only an occasional woodcutter passes by.
Once I was his pupil, a youth with shaggy hair,
Learning deeply from him by the Narrow River.
One morning I set off on my solitary journey
And the years passed between us in silence.
Now I have returned to find him at rest here;
How can I honour his departed spirit?
I pour a dipper of pure water over his tombstone
And offer a silent prayer.
The sun suddenly disappears behind the hill
And I'm enveloped by the roar of the wind in the pines.
I try to pull myself away but cannot;
A flood of tears soaks my sleeves.

In my youth I put aside my studies
And I aspired to be a saint.
Living austerey as a mendicant monk,
I wandered here and there for many springs.
Finally I returned home to settle under a craggy peak.
I live peacefully in a grass hut,
Listening to the birds for music.

Clouds are my best neighbours.
Below a pure spring where I refresh body and mind;
Above, towering pines and oaks that provide shade and
    brushwood.
Free, so free, day after day—
I never want to leave!

Yes, I'm truly a dunce
Living among trees and plants.
Please don't question me about illusion and
    enlightenment—
This old fellow just likes to smile to himself.
I wade across streams with bony legs,
And carry a bag about in fine spring weather.
That's my life,
And the world owes me nothing.

When all thoughts
Are exhausted
I slip into the woods
And gather
A pile of shepherd's purse.

Like the little stream
Making its way
Through the mossy crevices
I, too, quietly
Turn clear and transparent.

At dusk
I often climb
To the peak of Kugami.
Deer bellow,
Their voices
Soaked up by
Piles of maple leaves
Lying undisturbed at
The foot of the mountain.

Blending with the wind,
Snow falls;
Blending with the snow,
The wind blows.
By the hearth
I stretch out my legs,
Idling my time away
Confined in this hut.
Counting the days,
I find that February, too,
Has come and gone
Like a dream.

No luck today on my mendicant rounds;
From village to village I dragged myself.
At sunset I find myself with miles of mountains
between me and my hut.

The wind tears at my frail body,
And my little bowl looks so forlorn—
Yes this is my chosen path that guides me
Through disappointment and pain, cold and hunger.

— Ryokan

Eaten alive by
lice and fleas—now the horse
beside my pillow pees.

— Basho

I cam to realise that mind is no other than mountains
and rivers and the great wide earth, the sun and the
moon and the stars

— Dogen

For those who proclaim
they've grown weary of children,
there are no flowers.

— *Basho*

When I was a lad,
I sauntered about town as a gay blade,
Sporting a cloak of the softest down,
And mounted on a splendid chestnut-coloured horse.
During the day, I galloped to the city;
At night, I got drunk on peach blossoms by the river.
I never cared about returning home,
Usually ending up, with a big smile on my face, at a
pleasure pavilion!

Returning to my native village after many years' absence:
I put up at a country inn and listen to the rain.
One robe, one bowl is all I have.
I light incense and strain to sit in meditation;
All night a steady drizzle outside the dark window—
Inside, poignant memories of these long years of
pilgrimage.

— *Ryokan*

Emptiness is a name for nothingness,
A name for ungraspibility,
A name for mountains, rivers, the whole earth.
It is also called the real form.
In the green of the pines,
The twist of the brambles,
There is no going and coming;
In the red of the flowers
And the white of the snow,
There is no birth and no death.

— Ryusai

A master's handiwork cannot be measured
But still priests wag their tongues explaining the "Way"
and babbling about "Zen."
This old monk has never cared for false piety
And my nose wrinkles at the dark smell of incense
before the Buddha.

— Ryusai

Nothing in the cry
of cicadas suggests they
are about to die.

— Basho

He threw the coin into the air and all watched
intently as it landed. It was heads. The soldiers were so
overjoyed and filled with confidence that they
vigorously attacked the enemy and were victorious.
After the battle, a lieutenant remarked to the general,
"No one can change destiny."

"Quite right," the general replied as he showed the
lieutenant the coin, which had heads on both sides.

An autumn night—
don't think your life
didn't matter.

— Basho

The Mysterious

One Reality only—
How deep and far-reaching!
The ten thousand things—
How confusingly multifarious!

The true and the conventional are indeed
    intermingling,
But essentially of the same substance they are.

The wise and the unenlightened are indeed
    distinguishable,
But in the Way they are united as one.

Desirest thou to find its limits?
How broadly expanding! It is limitless!
How vaguely it vanishes away! Its ends are never
    reached!
It originates in beginningless time, it terminates in
endless time.

— *Seng Ts'an*

Guidepost of Silent Illumination

Silent and serene, forgetting words, bright clarity appears before you.

When you reflect it you become vast, where you embody it you are spiritually uplifted.

Spiritually solitary and shining, inner illumination restores wonder,

Dew in the moonlight, a river of stars, snow-covered pines, clouds enveloping the peaks.

In darkness it is most bright, while hidden all the more manifest.

The crane dreams in the wintry mists. The autumn waters flow far in the distance.

Endless kalpas are totally empty, all things are completely the same.

When wonder exists in serenity, all achievement is forgotten in illumination.

What is this wonder? Alertly seeing through confusion

Is the way of silent illumination and the origin of subtle radiance.

Vision penetrating into subtle radiance is weaving gold on a jade loom.

Upright and inclined yield to each other; light and dark are interdependent.

Not depending on sense faculty and object, at the right
time they interact.
Drink the medicine of good views. Beat the poison-
  smeared drum.
When they interact, killing and giving life are up to you.
Through the gate the self emerges and the branches
  bear fruit.
Only silence is the supreme speech, only illumination
  the universal response.
Responding without falling into achievement, speaking
  without involving listeners.
The ten thousand forms majestically glisten and
  expound the dharma.
All objects certify it, every one in dialogue.
Dialoguing and certifying, they respond appropriately
  to each other;
But if illumination neglects serenity then aggresiveness
  appears.
Certifying and dialoguing, they respond to each
  other appropriately;
But if serenity neglects illumination, murkiness leads to
  wasted dharma.
The silent illumination is fulfiled, the lotus blossoms,
  the dreamer awakens,
A hundred streams flow into the ocean, a thousand
  ranges face the highest peak.

Like geese preferring milk, like bees gathering nectar,
When silent illumination reaches the ultimate, I offer
    my teaching.
The teaching of silent illumination penetrates from the
    highest down to the foundation.
The body being shunyata, the arms in mudra,
From beginning to end the changing appearances and
    then thousand differences share one pattern.
Mr. Ho offered jade [to the Emperor]; [Minister]
    Xiangru pointed to its flaws.
Facing changes has its principles, the great function is
    without striving.
The ruler stays in the kingdom, the general goes
    beyond the frontiers.
Our school's affair hits the mark straight and true.
Transmit it to all directions without desiring to gain
    credit.

— *Hongzhi Zhengjue*

A university professor went to visit a famous Zen master. While the master quietly served tea, the professor talked about Zen. The master poured the visitor's cup to the brim, and then kept pouring. The professor watched the overflowing cup until he could no longer restrain himself. "It's over-full! No more will go in!" the professor blurted. "You are like this cup," the master replied, "How can I show you Zen unless you first empty your cup."

The great master Chuang Tzu once dreamt that he was a butterfly fluttering here and there. In the dream he had no awareness of his individuality as a person. He was only a butterfly. Suddenly, he awoke and found himself laying there, a person once again. But then he thought to himself, "Was I before a man who dreamt about being a butterfly, or am I now a butterfly who dreams about being a man?"

Song of the Grass-Roof Hermitage

I've built a grass hut where there's nothing of value.
After eating I relax and enjoy a nap.
When it was completed, fresh weeds appeared.
Now it's been lived in—covered by weeds.

The person in the hut lives here calmly,
Not stuck to inside, outside, or in between.
Places worldly people live, he doesn't live.
Realms worldly people love, he doesn't love.

Though the hut is small, it includes the entire world.
In ten square feet, an old man illumines forms and
    their nature.
A Great Vehicle bodhisattva trusts without doubt.
he middling or lowly can't help wondering;
Will this hut perish or not?

Perishable or not, the original master is present,
Not dwelling south or north, east or west.
Firmly based on steadiness, it can't be surpassed.
A shining window below the green pines—
Jade palaces or vermilion towers can't compare with it.

Just sitting with head covered, all things are at rest.
Thus, this mountain monk doesn't understand at all.
Living here he no longer works to get free.
Who would proudly arrange seats, trying to entice
     guests?

Turn around the light to shine within, then just return.
The vast inconceivable source can't be faced or turned
     away from.
Meet the ancestral teachers, be familiar with their
     instruction,
Bind grasses to build a hut, and don't give up.

Let go of hundreds of years and relax completely.
Open your hands and walk, innocent.
Thousands of words, myriad interpretations,
Are only to free you from obstructions.
If you want to know the undying person in the hut,
Don't separate from this skin bag here and now.

— *Shitou Xiqian*

This treasure was discovered in a bamboo thicket—
I washed the bowl in a spring and then mended it.
After morning meditation, I take my gruel in it;
At night, it serves me soup or rice.
Cracked, worn, weather-beaten, and misshapen
But still of noble stock!

Midsummer—
I walk about with my staff.
Old farmers spot me
And call me over for a drink.
We sit in the fields
Using leaves for plates.
Pleasantly drunk and so happy
I drift off peacefully
Sprawled out on a paddy bank.

How can I possibly sleep
This moonlit evening?
Come, my friends,
Let's sing and dance
All night long.

Stretched out,
Tipsy,
Under the vast sky:
Splendid dreams
Beneath the cherry blossoms.

Wild roses,
Plucked from fields,
Full of croaking frogs:
Float them in your wine
And enjoy every minute!

Heaven and earth and I are of the same root, the ten-thousand things and I are of one substance.

— *Sêng-chao/Sōjō*

Infinitely large and infinitely small; no difference, for definitions have vanished and no boundaries are seen.

A Meal of Fresh Octopus

Lots of arms, just like Kannon the Goddess;
Sacrificed for me, garnished with citron, I revere it so!
The taste of the sea, just divine!
Sorry, Buddha, this is another precept I just cannot
      keep.

Exhausted with gay pleasures, I embrace my wife.
The narrow path of asceticism is not for me:
My mind runs in the opposite direction.
It is easy to be glib about Zen—I'll just keep my
      mouth shut
And rely on love play all the day long.

It is nice to get a glimpse of a lady bathing—
You scrubbed your flower face and cleansed your lovely
      body
While this old monk sat in the hot water,
Feeling more blessed than even the emperor of China!

— *Ryokan*

The Buddha's Essential Functioning

The Buddha's essential functioning,
the patriarch's functioning essence,
Knows without relating to things
and illuminates without reflecting upon objects.
Knowing without relating to things,
its knowing is subtle of itself.
Illuminating without reflecting upon objects,
its illumination is mysterious of itself.
Its knowing, subtle of itself,
is the thought with no discrimination.
Its illumination, mysterious of itself,
is the sign without the slightest mark.
The thought with no discrimination,
its knowing is completed without other.
The sign without the slightest mark,
its illumination is revealed without choice.
The water is pure and clear to the bottom;
a fish swims slowly.
The sky is vast and finds no boundary;
a bird flies far away.

— Hongzhi Zhengjue

The Song of Zazen

All sentient beings are essentially Buddhas.
As with water and ice, there is no ice without water;
apart from sentient beings, there are no Buddhas.
Not knowing how close the truth is,
we seek it far away
—what a pity!

We are like one who in the midst of water cries out
    desperately in thirst.
We are like the son of a rich man who wandered away
    among the poor.
The reason we transmigrate through the Six Realms
is because we are lost in the darkness of ignorance.
Going further and further astray in the darkness,
how can we ever be free from birth-and-death?

As for the Mahayana practice of zazen,
there are no words to praise it fully.
The Six Paramitas,
such as giving, maintaining the precepts,
and various other good deeds
like invoking the Buddha's name,
repentance, and spiritual training,
all finally return to the practice of zazen.

Even those who have sat zazen only once will see all
  karma erased.
Nowhere will they find evil paths,
and the Pure Land will not be far away.
If we listen even once with open heart to this truth,
then praise it and gladly embrace it,
how much more so then,
if on reflecting within ourselves we directly realise
  Self-nature,
giving proof to the truth that Self-nature is no-nature.

We will have gone far beyond idle speculation.
The gate of the oneness of cause and effect is thereby
  opened,
and not-two, not-three,
straight ahead runs the Way.

Realising the form of no-form as form,
whether going or returning we cannot be any place
  else.
Realising the thought of no-thought as thought,
whether singing or dancing,
we are the voice of the Dharma.

How vast and wide the unobstructed sky of samadhi!
How bright and clear the perfect moonlight of the
Fourfold Wisdom!

At this moment what more need we seek?
As the eternal tranquillity of Truth reveals itself to us,
this very place is the land of Lotuses
and this very body
is the body of the Buddha.

— *Hakuin Ekaku Zenji*

One day Chuang Tzu and a friend were walking by a river. "Look at the fish swimming about," said Chuang Tzu, "They are really enjoying themselves."

"You are not a fish," replied the friend, "So you can't truly know that they are enjoying themselves."

"You are not me," said Chuang Tzu. "So how do you know that I do not know that the fish are enjoying themselves?"

A snowy heron
on the snowfield
where winter grass is unseen
hides itself
in its own figure.

Flowers In Our Eyes

How wonderful! The Buddhas throughout the ten directions
Are originally just the flowers in our eyes.
And if we want to know about these flowers in our eyes
They are originally the Buddhas throughout the ten directions.
If we want to know the Buddhas of the ten directions,
They are not flowers in our eyes.
If we want to know the flowers in our eyes,
They are not the Buddhas of the ten directions.
If you can understand this,
The Buddhas of the ten directions are to blame.
If you don't understand,
Those with only hear-say knowledge do a little dance,
And those who make up their own enlightenment put on make up.

— Guangzhou

If you try to aim for it, you are turning away from it.

— Zen master.

For Children Killed in a Smallpox Epidemic

When spring arrives
From every tree tip
Flowers will bloom,
But those children
Who fell with last autumn's leaves
Will never return.

I watch people in the world
Throw away their lives lusting after things,
Never able to satisfy their desires,
Falling into deeper despair
And torturing themselves.
Even if they get what they want
How long will they be able to enjoy it?
For one heavenly pleasure
They suffer ten torments of hell,
Binding themselves more firmly to the grindstone.
Such people are like monkeys
Frantically grasping for the moon in the water
And then falling into a whirlpool.
How endlessly those caught up in the floating world
    suffer.
Despite myself, I fret over them all night
And cannot staunch my flow of tears.

The wind has settled, the blossoms have fallen;
Birds sing, the mountains grow dark—
This is the wondrous power of Buddhism.

In a dilapidated three-room hut
I've grown old and tired;
This winter cold is the
Worst I've ever suffered through.
I sip thin gruel, waiting for the
Freezing night to pass.
Can I last until spring finally arrives?
Unable to beg for rice,
How will I survive the chill?
Even meditation helps no longer;
Nothing left to do but compose poems
In memory of deceased friends.

— *Ryokan*

I won't even stop
at the valley's brook
for fear that
my shadow
may flow into the world.

Awake or Asleep

Awake or asleep
in a grass hut,
what I pray for is
to bring others across
before myself.

Although this ignorant self
may never become a buddha
I vow to bring
others across
because I am a monk.

How august!
Studying the old words
of the Seven Buddhas
you pass beyond
the six realms.

The full-grown man aspires to pierce through the heavens: Let him not walk in the footsteps of the Buddha!

— *Ts'ui-yen*

The worthies of old all had
means of emancipating people.
What I teach people just requires
you not to take on the confusion of others.
If you need to act, then act,
without any further hesitation or doubt.

— Lin Chi

A Zen Master lived the simplest kind of life in a little
hut at the foot of a mountain. One evening, while he
was away, a thief sneaked into the hut only to find
there was nothing in it to steal. The Zen Master
returned and found him. "You have come a long way to
visit me," he told the prowler, "and you should not
return empty handed. Please take my clothes as a gift."
The thief was bewildered, but he took the clothes and
ran away. The Master sat naked, watching the moon.
"Poor fellow," he mused, "I wish I could give him this
beautiful moon."

Few people believe their
Inherent mind is Buddha.
Most will not take this seriously,
And therefore are cramped.
They are wrapped up in illusions, cravings,
Resentments, and other afflictions,
All because they love the cave of ignorance.

— Fenyang

Everything is
A lie in this world
Because even
Death
Isn't so.

When love and hate are both absent everything
becomes clear and undisguised.

The secret of the receptive
Must be sought in stillness;
Within stillness there remains
The potential for action.
If you force empty sitting,
Holding dead images in mind,
The tiger runs, the dragon flees—
How can the elixir be given?

The Perfect Way knows no difficulties
Except that it refuses to make preferences;
Only when freed from hate and love,
It reveals itself fully and without disguise;
A tenth of an inch's difference,
And heaven and earth are set apart;
If you wish to see it before your own eyes,
Have no fixed thoughts either for or against it.

— Sosan Canchi Zenji

Manjusri, a bodhisattva should regard all living
beings as a wise man
Regards the reflection of the moon in water,
As magicians regard men created by magic.
As being like a face in a mirror,
like the water of a mirage;
like the sound of an echo;
like a mass of clouds in the sky;
like the appearance and disappearance of a bubble of
   water;
like the core of a plantain tree;
like a flash of lightning;
like the appearance of matter in an immaterial realm;
like a sprout from a rotten seed;
like a tortoise-hair coat;
like the fun of games for one who wishes to die...

— *Vimalakirti Nirdesa Sutra*

Crossing long fields,
frozen in its saddle,
my shadow creeps by.

Enlightenment is like the moon reflected on the
water.
The moon does not get wet, nor is the water broken.
Although its light is wide and great,
The moon is reflected even in a puddle an inch wide.
The whole moon and the entire sky
Are reflected in one dewdrop on the grass.

— *Dogen*

It is as though you have an eye
That sees all forms
But does not see itself.
This is how your mind is.
Its light penetrates everywhere
And engulfs everything,
So why does it not know itself?

— *Foyan*

Speech is blasphemy, silence a lie. Above speech and
silence there is a way out.

— *I-tuan*

A monk set off on a long pilgrimage to find the Buddha. He devoted many years to his search until he finally reached the land where the Buddha was said to live. While crossing the river to this country, the monk looked around as the boatman rowed. He noticed something floating towards them. As it got closer, he realised that it was the corpse of a person. When it drifted so close that he could almost touch it, he suddenly recognised the dead body—it was his own! He lost all control and wailed at the sight of himself, still and lifeless, drifting along the river's currents. That moment was the beginning of his liberation.

Spring-water in the green creek is clear
Moonlight on Cold Mountain is white
Silent knowledge—the spirit is enlightened of itself
Contemplate the void: this world exceeds stillness.

— *Han-shan*

Asked "What is Buddha?"
Ma-tsu replied "This very mind, this is Buddha."

In spring wind
peach blossoms
begin to come apart.
Doubts do not grow
branches and leaves.

Water birds
going and coming
their traces disappear
but they never
forget their path.

Those who see worldly life as an obstacle to Dharma
see no Dharma in everyday actions.
They have not yet discovered that
there are no everyday actions outside of Dharma.

— Dogen

Who is hearing?
Your physical being doesn't hear,
Nor does the void.
Then what does?
Strive to find out.
Put aside your rational Intellect,
Give up all techniques.
Just get rid of the notion of self.

— Bassui

Hell is not punishment,
it's training.

— Shunryu Suzuki

The most important thing is to find out
what is the most important thing.

— Shunryu Suzuki

Well versed in the Buddha way,
I go the non-Way
Without abandoning my
Ordinary person's affairs.

The conditioned and
Name-and-form,
All are flowers in the sky.

Nameless and formless,
I leave birth-and-death.

— *Layman P'ang*

If you want to be free,
Get to know your real self.
It has no form, no appearance,
No root, no basis, no abode,
But is lively and buoyant.
It responds with versatile facility,
But its function cannot be located.
Therefore when you look for it,
You become further from it;
When you seek it,
You turn away from it all the more.

— *Linji*

Where beauty is, then there is ugliness;
where right is, also there is wrong.
Knowledge and ignorance are interdependent;
delusion and enlightenment condition each other.
Since olden times it has been so.
How could it be otherwise now?
Wanting to get rid of one and grab the other
is merely realising a scene of stupidity.
Even if you speak of the wonder of it all,
how do you deal with each thing changing?

— *Ryokan*

The monkey is reaching
For the moon in the water.
Until death overtakes him
He'll never give up.
If he'd let go the branch and
Disappear in the deep pool,
The whole world would shine
With dazzling pureness.

— *Hakuin*

The past is already past.
Don't try to regain it.
The present does not stay.
Don't try to touch it.

From moment to moment.
The future has not come;
Don't think about it
Beforehand.

Whatever comes to the eye,
Leave it be.
There are no commandments
To be kept;
There's no filth to be cleansed.

With empty mind really
Penetrated, the dharmas
Have no life.

When you can be like this,
You've completed
The ultimate attainment.

—*Layman P'ang*

A renowned Zen master said that his greatest teaching was this: Buddha is your own mind. So impressed by how profound this idea was, one monk decided to leave the monastery and retreat to the wilderness to meditate on this insight. There he spent 20 years as a hermit probing the great teaching.

One day he met another monk who was travelling through the forest. Quickly the hermit monk learned that the traveller also had studied under the same Zen master. "Please, tell me what you know of the master's greatest teaching." The traveller's eyes lit up, "Ah, the master has been very clear about this. He says that his greatest teaching is this: Buddha is NOT your own mind."

Just stop your wandering,
Look penetratingly into your inherent nature,
And, concentrating your spiritual energy,
Sit in zazen
And break through.

— *Bassui*

Whether you are going or staying or sitting or lying
   down,
the whole world is your own self.
You must find out
whether the mountains, rivers, grass, and forests
exist in your own mind or exist outside it.
Analyse the ten thousand things,
dissect them minutely,
and when you take this to the limit
you will come to the limitless,
when you search into it you come to the end of search,
where thinking goes no further and distinctions vanish.
When you smash the citadel of doubt,
then the Buddha is simply yourself.

— *Daikaku*

However deep your
Knowledge of the scriptures,
It is no more than a strand of hair
In the vastness of space;
However important appears
Your worldly experience,
It is but a drop of water in a deep ravine.

— *Tokusan*

If you have never taken
The principles of the teachings to heart,
You have no basis
For awakening to the hidden path.

— Kuei-shan Ling-yu

When mortals are alive, they worry about death.
When they're full, they worry about hunger.
Theirs is the Great Uncertainty.

But sages don't consider the past.
And they don't worry about the future.
Nor do they cling to the present.
And from moment to moment they follow the Way.

— Bodhidharma

Waves recede.
Not even the wind ties up
a small abandoned boat.
the moon is a clear
mark of midnight.

The bee emerging
from deep within the peony
departs reluctantly.

— *Basho*

What is this mind?
Who is hearing these sounds?
Do not mistake any state for
Self-realisation, but continue
To ask yourself even more intensely,
What is it that hears?

— *Bassui*

Where there is great doubt,
there will be great awakening;
small doubt, small awakening,
no doubt, no awakening.

Shuzan held out his short staff and said, "If you call
this a short staff, you oppose its reality. If you do not
call it a short staff, you ignore the fact. Now what do
you wish to call this?"

Cast off what has been realised.
Turn back to the subject
That realises
To the root bottom
And resolutely
Go on.

— *Bassui*

Food and clothes sustain
Body and life;
I advise you to learn
Being as is.
When it's time,
I move my hermitage and go,
And there's nothing
To be left behind.

— Layman P'ang

Good and evil have no self nature;
Holy and unholy are empty names;
In front of the door is the land of stillness and quiet;
Spring comes, grass grows by itself.

— Master Seung Sahn

The thief
Left it behind—
The moon at the window.

— Ryokan

Upon meeting a Zen master at a social event, a psychiatrist decided to ask him a question that had been on his mind. "Exactly how do you help people?" he inquired.

"I get them to where they can't ask any more questions," the Master answered.

To what shall
I liken the world?
Moonlight, reflected
In dewdrops.
Shaken from a crane's bill.

— *Dogen*

Make the smallest distinction, however, and heaven and earth are set infinitely apart.

This is what should be done
By one who is skilled in goodness,
And who knows the path of peace:
Let them be able and upright,
Straightforward and gentle in speech.
Humble and not conceited,
Contented and easily satisfied.
Unburdened with duties and frugal in their ways.
Peaceful and calm, and wise and skillful,
Not proud and demanding in nature.
Let them not do the slightest thing
That the wise would later reprove.

> — *The Buddha's Words on*
> *Kindness (Metta Sutta)*

Reciting a small portion of the scriptures,
But putting it diligently into practice;
Letting go of passion, aggression, and confusion:
Revering the truth with a clear mind;
And not clinging to anything, here or hereafter;
Brings the harvest of the holy life.

> — *Dhammapada*

How boundless the cleared sky of Samadhi!
How transparent the perfect moonlight of the Fourfold
    Wisdom!
At this moment what more need we seek?
As the Truth eternally reveals itself,
This very place is the Lotus Land of Purity,
This very body is the Body of the Buddha.

                     — *Hakuin Ekaku Zenji*

Opening bell
echoes from the canyon walls—
raindrops on the river.
The sounds of rocks bouncing off rocks;
the shadows of trees traced on trees.

I sit, still.
The canyon river chants,
moving mountains.

The sermon spun on the still point:
dropping off eternity, picking up time;
letting go of self, awakened to Mind.

My daily activities are not unusual,
I'm just naturally in harmony with them.
Grasping nothing, discarding nothing...
Supernatural power and marvellous activity—
Drawing water and carrying firewood.

— *Pang-yun*

The wind has settled, the blossoms have fallen;
Birds sing, the mountains grow dark—
This is the wondrous power of Buddhism.

— *Ryokan*

Old pond,
frog jumps in
—splash

— *Basho*

No tranquilization, No disturbance,
No sitting, No meditation...
This is the Tathagata's Dhyana.
The five Skandhas are not realities;
The six object of sense are by nature empty.
It is neither quiet nor illuminating;
It is neither real nor empty;
It does not abide in the Middle Way;
It is not-doing,
It is no-effect-producing;
Yet, functioning with the utmost freedom:
the Buddha-nature is all inclusive.

— *Hui-neng*

Look directly!
What is this?
Look in this manner
And you won't be fooled!

— *Bassui*

If you ignore its profundity,
you can never practice stillness.
Like the Great Void, it is Perfect and lacks nothing,
nor has any excess.
If you discriminate,
you will miss its suchness.
Cling not to external causes,
nor stay in the Void.
Differentiation ceases if you can be impartial.
Stillness comes when all disturbances are stopped,
clinging to stillness is also a mistake.
If you cling to opposites,
how will you know the One?

However looked at,
it's a world
to be loathed—
but as long as you live here
I'm drawn to it!
                                    — *Saigyo*

All that's visible springs from causes intimate to you.
While walking, sitting, lying down, the body itself is
   complete truth.
If someone asks the inner meaning of this:
"Inside the treasury of the dharma eye a single grain of
   dust."
                        — *Dogen*

Only the idea of self remains
Floating on a sea of cells;
Only heartbeats short of eternity
In breath after breath we dwell.

Look for Buddha outside your own mind,
and Buddha becomes the devil.
                        — *Dogen*

Though I think not
To think about it,
I do think about it
And shed tears
Thinking about it.

— Ryokan

Nobly, the great priest
deposits his daily stool
in bleak winter fields.

— Buson

A life-time is not what's between,
The moments of birth and death.
A life-time is one moment,
Between my two little breaths.

The present, the here, the now,
That's all the life I get,
I live each moment in full,
In kindness, in peace, without regret.

— Chade Meng

In the awakened eye
Mountains and rivers
Completely disappear.
The eye of delusion
Gazes upon
Deep fog and clouds.
Alone in my zazen
I forget the days
As they pass.
The wisteria has grown
Thick over the eaves
Of my hut.

— *Muso*

New leaves
On a tree
Thought dead.

In ten directions everywhere, throughout the sea of
   lands,
Every hair-tip encompasses oceans of past, present and
   future.
So, too, there is a sea of Buddhas, a sea of Buddha
   lands;
Pervading them all, I cultivate for seas of endless time.

The water and my mind have both settled down
Into perfect stillness.
Sun and moon shine bright in it.

At night I see in the surface
The enormous face of my old familiar moon.
I don't think you've ever met the source of this
   reflection.

All shrillness fades into the sound of silence.
But now and then a puff of mist floats across the
   mirror.

It confuses me a little
But not enough to make me forget to forget my cares.

— *Master Hsu Yun*

To study the Buddha way is to study the self.
To study the self is to forget the self.
To forget the self is to be enlightened by the ten
   thousand dharmas.
To be enlightened by the ten thousand dharmas is to
   free one's body and mind and those of others.
No trace of enlightenment remains, and this traceless
   enlightenment is continued forever.

— Dogen

But I say unto you,
Take this staff just as a staff;
Movement is movement;
Sitting is sitting,
   but don't wobble
   under any circumstances!
My staff has turned into a dragon
   and swallowed up the whole world.
Where are the poor mountains and rivers and great
   earth now?

If you are a poet, you will see clearly that there is a
cloud floating in this
sheet of paper. Without a cloud there will be no
water; without water,
the trees cannot grow; and without trees, you cannot
make paper. So
the cloud is in here. The existence of this page is
dependent upon the
existence of a cloud. Paper and cloud are so close.

— *Thich Nhat Hahn*

Before I had studied Zen for thirty years,
I saw mountains as mountains, and waters as waters.
When I arrived at a more intimate knowledge, I came
to the point
where I saw that mountains are not mountains,
and waters are not waters.
But now that I have got its very substance I am at rest.
For it's just that I see mountains once again as
mountains, and waters once again as waters.

— *Ching-yuan*

Shariputra,
Form does not differ from emptiness;
Emptiness does not differ from form.
Form itself is emptiness;
Emptiness itself is form.
So too are feeling, cognition, formation,
and consciousness.

— *Heart Sutra*

As flowing waters disappear into the mist
We lose all track of their passage.
Every heart is its own Buddha.
Ease off... become immortal.

Wake up! The world's a mote of dust.
Behold heaven's round mirror.
Turn loose! Slip past shape and shadow,
Sit side by side with nothing, save Tao.

— *Shih-shu*

The mind of the past is ungraspable;
the mind of the future is ungraspable;
the mind of the present is ungraspable.

— *Diamond Sutra*

A world of dew,
and within every dewdrop
a world of struggle.

— *Issa*

Unfettered at last, a travelling monk,
I pass the old Zen barrier.
Mine is a traceless stream-and-cloud life,
Of these mountains, which shall be my home?

—*Manan*

If you want to climb a mountain, begin at the top.

Harmony of Difference and Sameness

The mind of the great sage of India
is intimately transmitted from west to east.
While human faculties are sharp or dull,
the Way has no northern or southern ancestors.
The spiritual source shines clear in the light;
the branching streams flow on in the dark.
Grasping at things is surely delusion;
according with sameness is still not enlightenment.
All the objects of the senses
interact and yet do not.
Interacting brings involvement.
Otherwise, each keeps its place.
Sights vary in quality and form,
sounds differ as pleasing or harsh.
Refined and common speech come together in the
    dark,
clear and murky phrases are distinguished in the light.
The four elements return to their natures
just as a child turns to its mother;
Fire heats, wind moves,
water wets, earth is solid.
Eye and sights, ear and sounds,
nose and smells, tongue and tastes;
Thus with each and every thing,

depending on these roots, the leaves spread forth.
Trunk and branches share the essence;
revered and common, each has its speech.
In the light there is darkness,
but don't take it as darkness;
In the dark there is light,
but don't see it as light.
Light and dark oppose one another
like the front and back foot in walking.
Each of the myriad things has its merit,
expressed according to function and place.
Phenomena exist; box and lid fit;
principle responds; arrow points meet.
Hearing the words, understand the meaning;
don't set up standards of your own.
If you don't understand the Way right before you,
how will you know the path as you walk?
Progress is not a matter of far or near,
but if you are confused, mountains and rivers block
    your way.
I respectfully urge you who study the mystery,
do not pass your days and nights in vain.

The mind is an organ of thought and objects are set
   against it:
The two are like marks on the surface of the mirror;
When the dirt is removed, the light begins to shine.
Both mind and objects being forgotten, Ultimate Nature
   reveals itself true.

— *Yung-chia Hsüan-chüeh*

As the pines grew old and the clouds idled
He found boundless contentment within himself.

— *Babo*

There is no beginning to practice
nor end to enlightenment;
There is no beginning to enlightenment
nor end to practice.

— *Dogen*

A hermit was meditating by a river when a young man interrupted him. "Master, I wish to become your disciple," said the man. "Why?" replied the hermit. The young man thought for a moment. "Because I want to find God."

The master jumped up, grabbed him by the scruff of his neck, dragged him into the river, and plunged his head under water. After holding him there for a minute, with him kicking and struggling to free himself, the master finally pulled him up out of the river. The young man coughed up water and gasped to get his breath. When he eventually quieted down, the master spoke. "Tell me, what did you want most of all when you were under water."

"Air!" answered the man.

"Very well," said the master. "Go home and come back to me when you want God as much as you just wanted air."

When I hear I see, when I see I hear.
                                    — *Zen koan*

Lightning:
Heron's cry
Stabs the darkness.

— *Basho*

Even though I'm in Kyoto,
when the kookoo cries,
I long for Kyoto.

— *Issa*

My legacy—
What will it be?
Flowers in spring,
The cuckoo in summer,
And the crimson maples
Of autumn...

— *Ryokan*

Finally out of reach—
No bondage, no dependency.
How calm the ocean,
Towering the void.

— *Tessho's death poem*

Loving old priceless things,
I've scorned those seeking
Truth outside themselves:
Here, on the tip of the nose.

— *Makusho*

Four monks decided to meditate silently without speaking for two weeks. By nightfall on the first day, the candle began to flicker and then went out. The first monk said, "Oh, no! The candle is out." The second monk said, "Aren't we not supposed to talk?" The third monk said, "Why must you two break the silence?" The fourth monk laughed and said, "Ha! I'm the only one who didn't speak."

Everything
just as it is,
as it is,
as is.
Flowers in bloom.
Nothing to add.

Fathomed at last!
Ocean's dried. Void burst.
Without an obstacle in sight,
It's everywhere!

— *Joho*

To wake in the present
Eat and work in the eternal now;
This is the way of the wise;
This is the path to the Absolute.

Enlightenment is basically not a tree,
And the clear mirror is not a stand.
Fundamentally there is not a single thing—
Where can dust collect.

— *Huineng, Sixth Zen Patriarch
in China*

There I was, hunched over office desk,
Mind an unruffled pool.
A thunderbolt! My middle eye
Shot wide, revealing—my ordinary self.

— *Seiken*

An explosive shout cracks the great empty sky.
Immediately clear self-understanding.
Swallow up buddhas and ancestors of the past.
Without following others, realise complete
    penetration.

— *Dogen*

Two come about because of One,
but don't cling to the One either!
So long as the mind does not stir,
the ten thousand things stay blameless;
no blame, no phenomena,
no stirring, no mind.

The viewer disappears along with the scene,
the scene follows the viewer into oblivion,
for scene becomes scene only through the viewer,
viewer becomes viewer because of the scene.

— Seng-ts'an

The Three Thousand Worlds
that step forward
with the light snow,
and the light snow that falls
in those Three Thousand Worlds.

— Ryokan

Gone, and a million things leave no trace
Loosed, and it flows through the galaxies
A fountain of light, into the very mind—
Not a thing, and yet it appears before me:
Now I know the pearl of the Buddha-nature
Know its use: a boundless perfect sphere.

         — *Han-Shan*

Earth, mountains, rivers—hidden in nothingness.
In this nothingness—earth, mountains, rivers revealed.
Spring flowers, winter snows:
There's no being or non-being, nor denial itself.

         — *Saisho*

A special transmission outside the scriptures;
No dependence upon words and letters;
Direct pointing at the soul of man:
Seeing into one's nature and the attainment of
     Buddhahood.

         — *Bodhi-Dharma*

Buddha preached in the twelve divisions,
each division full of purest truth.
East wind—rain comes in the night,
making all the forest fresh and new.
No sutra that does not save the living,
no branch in the forest not visited by spring.
Learn to understand the meaning in them,
don't try to decide which is "valid," which is not.

— *Ryokan*

Mind is the moment of actualising the fundamental
point; words are the moment of going beyond,
unlocking the barrier.
Arriving is the moment of casting off the body;
not-arriving is the moment of being one with just this,
while being free from just this. In this way you must
endeavour to actualise the time-being.

Studying texts and stiff meditation can make you lose
   your Original Mind.
A solitary tune by a fisherman, though, can be an
   invaluable treasure.
Dusk rain on the river, the moon peeking in and out of
   the clouds;
Elegant beyond words, he chants his songs night after
   night.

The world before my eyes is wan and wasted, just
   like me.
The earth is decrepit, the sky stormy, all the grass
   withered.
No spring breeze even at this late date,
Just winter clouds swallowing up my tiny reed hut.

Along the roadside,
blossoming wild roses
in my horse's mouth.

In this warm spring rain,
tiny leaves are sprouting
from the eggplant seed.

Zen opens a man's eyes to the greatest mystery as it
is daily and hourly performed; it enlarges the heart to
embrace eternity of time and infinity of space in its
every palpitation; it makes us live in the world as if
walking in the garden of Eden.

— *D. T. Suzuki*

Learning Zen is a phenomenon of gold and dung.
Before you understand it, it's like gold; after you
understand it, it's like dung.

— *Zen master*

One moon shows in every pool;
In every pool, the one moon.

— *Zen Forest Saying*

The Zen master Hakuin used to tell his students about an old woman who owned a tea shop in the village. She was skilled in the tea ceremony, Hakuin said, and her understanding of Zen was superb. Many students wondered about this and went to the village themselves to check her out. Whenever the old woman saw them coming, she could tell immediately whether they had come to experience the tea, or to probe her grasp of Zen. Those wanting tea she served graciously. For the others wanting to learn about her Zen knowledge, she hid until they approached her door and then attacked them with a fire poker. Only one out of ten managed to escape her beating.

The world is like a mirror, you see? Smile, and your friends smile back.

—Japanese Zen Saying

If you understand, things are just as they are...
if you do not understand, things are just as they are.

So an ancient once said, "Accept the anxieties and difficulties of this life". Don't expect your practice to be clear of obstacles. Without hindrances the mind that seeks enlightenment may be burnt out. So an ancient once said, "Attain deliverance in disturbances".

— *Zen Master Kyong Ho*

From the pine tree
learn of the pine tree
and from the bamboo
learn of the bamboo.

— *Basho*

Student says
I am very discouraged
what should I do?
Master says
encourage others.

If you cannot find the truth right where you are
where else do you expect to find it?

— *Dogen Zenji*

People born into this floating world
Quickly become like roadside dust:
At dawn, little children,
By sunset, white-haired and old,
With no inner understanding
They struggle without cease.
I ask the children of the universe,
Why do you bother to pass this way?

— *Ryokan*

A flower falls
even though we love it
and a weed grows
even though we do not love it.

— *Dogen Zenji*

Although you keep
A jewel within yourself,
Nobody will notice it
Unless you
Polish and brighten it.

Sitting quietly, doing nothing,
Spring comes, and the grass grows by itself.

— *Zenrin Kushû*

All conditioned things are impermanent
be a lamp unto yourself.

—*Buddha's last words*

Ocean of pure Reality, its substance, in fathomless
quiescence, exists eternally.

— *Fo-kuang Ju-man*

The body is the tree of enlightenment
the mind like a clear mirror stand
time and gain wipe it diligently
don't let it gather dust.

— Shenxiu

It is just like learning archery; eventually you reach a
point where ideas are ended and feelings forgotten,
and then you suddenly hit the target.

— Ying-an

Sharing a Mountain Hut with a Cloud

A lonely hut on the mountain-peak towering above a
   thousand others;
One half is occupied by an old monk and the other by
   a cloud:
Last night it was stormy and the cloud was blown away;
After all a cloud could not equal the old man's quiet way.

— Kuei-tsung Chih-chih

Reverence is
The source of divine favours;
Without it,
Buddhas and wooden clogs are
Only pieces of wood.

Our illusions are
The beginning of
Satori;
See how sour grapes
Become sweet raisins.

Commit not a single unwholesome action,
Cultivate a wealth of virtue,
To tame this mind of ours.
This is the teaching of all the buddhas.

— *Buddha*

If you do not get it from yourself,
Where will you go for it?

All existent phenomena are empty;
beware of taking as real,
all that is nonexistent.

> — *Layman P'ang*

A young man caught a small bird, and held it behind his back. He then asked, "Master, is the bird I hold in my hands alive or dead." The boy thought this was a grand opportunity to play a trick on the old man. If the master answered "dead", it would be let loose into the air. If the master answered "alive", he would simply wring its neck. The master spoke, "The answer is in your hands".

Everything the same;
everything distinct.

In my daily life there are no other chores than
Those that happen to fall into my hands.
Nothing I choose, nothing reject.
Nowhere is there ado, nowhere a slip.
I have no other emblems of my glory than
The mountains and hills without a spot of dust.
My magical power and spiritual exercise consists in
Carrying water and gathering firewood.

— *P'ang Chü-shih*

Stillness

The ten directions converging,
Each learning to do nothing,
This is the hall of Buddha's training;
Mind's empty, all's finished.

— *P'ang Yün*

Ears hear and eyes see,
What then does mind do?

When the spiritual teacher and his disciples began their evening meditation, the cat who lived in the monastery made such noise that it distracted them. So the teacher ordered that the cat be tied up during the evening practice. Years later, when the teacher died, the cat continued to be tied up during the meditation session. And when the cat eventually died, another cat was brought to the monastery and tied up. Centuries later, learned descendants of the spiritual teacher wrote scholarly treatises about the religious significance of tying up a cat for meditation practice.

Some there are that torment themselves afresh with the memory of what is past; others, again, afflict themselves with the apprehension of evils to come; and very ridiculously both—for the one does not now concern us, and the other not yet... One should count each day a separate life.

— *Seneca*

Mind at Peace

When the mind is at peace,
the world too is at peace.
Nothing real, nothing absent.
Not holding on to reality,
not getting stuck in the void,
you are neither holy or wise, just
an ordinary fellow who has completed his work.

— *P'ang Yün*

Mindfulness

Spring comes with its flowers, autumn with the
    moon,
summer with breezes, winter with snow;
when useless things don't stick in the mind,
that is your best season.

— *Wu-men Huai-kai*

The plum blossoms in
The basement emit fragrance;
Secret love will
Speak for itself.

What is this seed, a mustard
Or a poppy? It's hard to tell
Which is which.
But when fully grown,
The flowers will tell.

A luminous moon, the wind in the pine,
A long evening, a transcendent view:
But what is the meaning of this?
What is the meaning of life?

Old P'ang requires nothing in the world:
All is empty with him, even a seat he has not,
For absolute Emptiness reigns in his household;
How empty indeed it is with no treasures!
When the sun is risen, he walks through Emptiness,
When the sun sets, he sleeps in Emptiness;
Sitting in Emptiness he sings his empty songs,
And his empty songs reverberate through Emptiness:
Be not surprised at Emptiness so thoroughly empty,
For Emptiness is the seat of all the Buddhas;
And Emptiness is not understood by the men of the
    world,
But Emptiness is the real treasure:
If you say there's no Emptiness,
You commit grave offense against the Buddhas.

— *P'ang*

At Nantai I sit quietly with an incense burning,
One day of rapture, all things are forgotten,
Not that mind is stopped and thoughts are put away,
But that there is really nothing to disturb my serenity.

— *Shou-an*

A bird in a secluded grove sings like a flute.
Willows sway gracefully with their golden threads.
The mountain valley grows the quieter as the clouds
　　return.
A breeze brings along the fragrance of the apricot
　　flowers.
For a whole day I have sat here encompassed by peace,
Till my mind is cleansed in and out of all cares and idle
　　thoughts.
I wish to tell you how I feel, but words fail me.
If you come to this grove, we can compare notes.

— Ch'an master Fa-yen

Something there is, prior to heaven and earth,
Without form, without sound, all alone by itself.
It has the power to control all the changing things;
Yet it changes not in the course of the four seasons.

— Bodhisattva Shan-hui

One disciple was bragging about his master to the disciple of another master. He claims that his teacher is capable of all sorts of magical acts, like writing in the air with a brush, and having the characters appear on a piece of paper hundreds of feet away. "And what can YOUR master do?" he asks the other disciple. "My master can also perform amazing feats," the other student replies. "When he's tired, he sleeps. When hungry, he eats."

Though the many beings are numberless,
I vow to save them.
Though greed, hatred, and ignorance rise endlessly,
I vow to cut them off.
Though the Dharma is vast and fathomless,
I vow to understand it.
Though Buddha's Way is beyond attainment,
I vow to embody it fully.

On leaf and grass
Awaiting the morning sun
The dew melts quickly away.
Haste thee not, O autumn wind
Who dost now stir in the fields!

— Dõgen Kigen

Every day I'm either in a wine shop or a brothel,
A free-spirited monk who is hard to fathom;
My surplice always appears torn and dirty,
But when I patch it, it smells so sweet.

To learn Buddha Dharma is to learn the self.
To learn the self is to forget the self.
To forget the self is to become one with
endless dimension, Universal Mind.

— Dõgen

All beings by nature are Buddha,
As ice by nature is water.
Apart from water there is no ice;
Apart from beings, no Buddha.

How sad that people ignore the near
And search for truth afar:
Like someone in the midst of water
Crying out in thirst;
Like a child of a wealthy home
Wandering among the poor.

Lost on dark paths of ignorance,
We wander through the Six Worlds;
From dark path to dark path—
When shall we be freed from birth and death?

Oh, the zazen of the Mahayana!
To this the highest praise!
Devotion, repentance, training,
The many paramitas—
All have their source in zazen.

Those who try zazen even once
Wipe away beginningless crimes.
Where are all the dark paths then?
The Pure Land itself is near.

Those who hear this truth even once
And listen with a grateful heart,
Treasuring it, revering it,
Gain blessings without end.

Much more, those who turn about
And bear witness to self-nature,
Self-nature that is no-nature,
Go far beyond mere doctrine.

Here effect and cause are the same;
The Way is neither two nor three.
With form that is no-form,
Going and coming, we are never astray;
With thought that is no-thought,
Singing and dancing are the voice of the Law.

Boundless and free is the sky of Samadhi!
Bright the full moon of wisdom!
Truly, is anything missing now?
Nirvana is right here, before our eyes;
This very place is the Lotus Land;
This very body, the Buddha

— *Hakuin Zenji*

We eat, excrete, sleep, and get up;
This is our world.
All we have to do after that—
Is to die.

— *Dōka*

Old Pan Kou knows nothing about time
and nothing about space as well.
His life is self-natured and self-sufficient.
He needs to ask for nothing outside of his own being.
The genesis of the world is the exercise of his mind.
When his mind starts to think, the world starts to
   move.
The world has never been made by any special design.
Neither has an end ever been put to it.

I stroll along the stream up to where it ends.
I sit down watching the clouds as they begin to rise.

— *Wang Wei*

In the midsummer heat, the gate is closed and we're
    wearing monk's robes,
In addition, there are no pines or bamboos shading the
    rooms and corridors,
For a peaceful meditation, we need not to go to the
    mountains and streams;
When thoughts are quieted down, fire itself is cool and
    refreshing.

                              — Tu Kou-hao

Forgetting all knowledge at one stroke,
I do not need cultivation anymore.
Activity expressing the ancient road,
I don't fall into passivity.
Everywhere trackless,
conduct beyond sound and form:
the adepts in all places
call this the supreme state.

                        — Hsiang-yen Chih-hsien

You wish to know the spirit of Yung-ming Zen?
Look at the lake in front of the gate.
When the sun shines, it radiates light and brightness,
When the wind comes, there arise ripples and waves.

— *Yung-ming Yen-shou*

The spring mountains covered with layers of most
   variegated colours,
And the spring streams fancifully laden with the
   reflecting images.
Standing by himself between heaven and earth,
Facing infinitude of beings.

— *Hsüeh-t'ou Ch'ung-hsien*

Without a rope,
people bind
themselves.

One, seven, three, five.
What you search for cannot be grasped.
As the night deepens, the moon brightens over the
   ocean.
The black dragon's jewel is found in every wave.
Looking for the moon, it is here in this wave and the
   next.

— Hsueh-t'ou Ch'ung-hsien

The bamboo shadows are sweeping the stairs,
But no dust is stirred:
The moonlight penetrates deep in the bottom of the
   pool,
But no trace is left in the water.

While living, one sits up and lies not,
When dead, one lies and sits not;
A set of ill-smelling skeleton!
What is the use of toiling and moiling so?

— Hui-neng, T'an-ching

Monks sit peacefully among the trees,
Ridding themselves of illusion with a calm mind.
Quietly realising enlightenment,
They experience a joy that is beyond that of heaven.
Laymen seek fame and profit,
Or fine robes, seats, and bedding.
Though the joy in getting them is only fleeting,
They are untiring in their quest.
Monks, however, beg for food in humble robes,
Their daily actions being one with the Way.
With their Wisdom-eye opened
They realise the essence of the Law.
Gathering all together to listen
To the countless Buddhist teachings,
They leave behind the world of illusion,
Quietly enveloped in enlightenment's Wisdom.

— *Bodhisattva Nâgârjuna*

Detached
Be detached, be detached!
Be thoroughly detached!
What then?
The pine is green,
And white is the snow.

The heaven and earth afford me no shelter at all;
I'm glad, unreal are body and soul.
Welcome thy weapon, O warrior of Yuan! Thy trusty
  steel,
That flashes lightning, cuts the wind of Spring, I feel.

— *Wu-hsüeh Tsu-yüan*

A distraught man approached the Zen master.
"Please, Master, I feel lost, desperate. I don't know who
I am. Please, show me my true self!" But the teacher
just looked away without responding. The man began
to plead and beg, but still the master gave no reply.
Finally giving up in frustration, the man turned to
leave. At that moment the master called out to him by
name. "Yes!" the man said as he spun back around.
"There it is!" exclaimed the master.

There's nothing equal to wearing clothes and eating
food.

— *Zenrin Kushû*

The moon pours light
Across the stream abundantly.
The pines breathe softly.
Who is leading this sacred evening
Toward everlasting night?
Deep in his heart he wears the seal,
The flawless pearl of Buddha-nature.

Never regard this world as
The only one;
The next world
And the one after the next...
All the worlds are here now.

To go to
Heaven is
The very beginning of
Falling into hell.

One with It
Long seeking it through others,
I was far from reaching it.
Now I go by myself;
I meet it everywhere.
It is just I myself,
And I am not itself.
Understanding this way,
I can be as I am.

—Tung-shan Ling-chia

In a moonlit night on a spring day,
The croak of a frog
Pierces through the whole cosmos and turns it into
a single family!

— Chang Chiu-ch'en

No clinging, no seeking.

— Pai-chang

Don't seek from others,
Or you'll be estranged from yourself.
I now go on alone—
Everywhere I encounter It.
It now is me, I now am not It.
One must understand in this way
To merge with being as is.

I beg to urge you everyone:
life and death is a grave matter;
all things pass quickly away.
Each of you must be completely alert;
never neglectful, never indulgent.

I rebuke the wind and revile the rain,
I do not know the Buddhas and patriarchs;
My single activity turns in the twinkling of an eye,
Swifter even than a lightning flash.

— *Nanpo Jõmyõ*

The celestial radiance undimmed,
The norm lasting for ever more;
For him who entereth this gate,
No reasoning, no learning.

— *P'ing-t'ien P'u-an*

Here rules an absolute quietness, all doings subside;
Just a touch, and lo, a roaring thunder-clap!
A noise that shakes the earth, and all silence;
The skull is broken to pieces, and awakened I am from
the dream!

— *Tu-feng Chi-shan*

Buddhas and patriarchs cut to pieces;
The sword is ever kept sharpened.
Where the wheel turns,
The void gnashes its teeth.

Great mountains, rivers and seas,
Heaven and earth, sun and moon.
Who says there is no birth and death?
For even these meet their end soon.

— *Shun-tsung*

Birth is also before birth,
Death is also before death.
If you have attained no-mind,
Naturally there will be nothing left.

— *Ju-man*

This body is the Bodhi-tree,
The soul is like a mirror bright;
Take heed to keep it always clean,
And let no dust collect on it.

— *Shen-hsiu*

From where did the Buddha come,
To where did the Buddha go?
If the Buddha is still around,
Where can be the Buddha found?

— *Shun-tsung*

The wind traverses the vast sky,
clouds emerge from the mountains;
Feelings of enlightenment and things of the world
are of no concern at all.

— *Master Keizan Jōkin*

Empty-handed, I hold a hoe.
Walking on foot, I ride a buffalo.
Passing over a bridge, I see
The bridge flow, but not the water.

— *Bodhisattva Shan-hui*

There is a bright pearl within me,
Buried for a long time under dust.
Today, the dust is gone and the light radiates,
Shining through all the mountains and rivers.

— *Master Yueh of Ch'a-ling*

I, Wo-luan, know a device
Whereby to blot out all my thoughts:
The objective world no more stirs the mind,
And daily matures my Enlightenment!

— *Wo-luan*

May we extend this mind over all beings
so that we and the world together
may attain maturity in Buddha's wisdom.

It is better to practice a little than talk a lot.

— *Muso Kokushi*

Refraining from all evil, not clinging to birth and
death, working in deep compassion for all sentient
beings, respecting those over you and pitying those
below you, without any detesting or desiring,
worrying or lamentation—this is what is called
Buddha. Do not search beyond it.

— Dogen

Not to commit wrongs,
To practise good,
To help others and
Purify the mind;

If you're without an umbrella and get soaked,
why fight the shower? Remember the rain has it's job,
too—and who are we to stand in its way.

Your working life is an expression of what you believe
in, and how much good you desire to do in the world.

Keep your heart clear and transparent
And you will never be bound.
A single disturbed thought, though,
Creates ten thousand distractions.
Let myriad things captivate you
And you'll go further and further astray.
How painful to see people
All wrapped up.

To what shall I compare this life of ours?
Even before I can say
it is like a lightning flash or a dewdrop
it is no more.

— *Sengai*

A rich man asked a Zen master to write something down that could encourage the prosperity of his family for years to come. It would be something that the family could cherish for generations. On a large piece of paper, the master wrote, "Father dies, son dies, grandson dies."

The rich man became angry when he saw the master's work. "I asked you to write something down that could bring happiness and prosperity to my family. Why do you give me something depressing like this?"

"If your son should die before you," the master answered, "this would bring unbearable grief to your family. If your grandson should die before your son, this also would bring great sorrow. If your family, generation after generation, disappears in the order I have described, it will be the natural course of life. This is true happiness and prosperity."

Don't seek reality, just put an end to opinions.
— *Sheng-ts'an*

Void is Form
When, just as they are,
White dewdrops gather
On scarlet maple leaves,
Regard the scarlet beads!

Form is Void
The tree is stripped,
All colour, fragrance gone,
Yet already on the bough,
Uncaring spring!

— *Ikkyu*

A martial arts student approached his teacher with a question. "I'd like to improve my knowledge of the martial arts. In addition to learning from you, I'd like to study with another teacher in order to learn another style. What do you think of this idea?"

"The hunter who chases two rabbits," answered the master, "catches neither one."

There is a reality even prior to heaven and earth;
Indeed, it has no form, much less a name;
Eyes fail to see it;
It has no voice for ears to detect;
To call it Mind or Buddha violates its nature,
For it then becomes like a visionary flower in the air;
It is not Mind, nor Buddha;
Absolutely quiet, and yet illuminating in a mysterious
    way,
It allows itself to be perceived only by the clear-eyed.

— *Daio Kokushi*

Bitter rain soaks the pile of kindling twigs.
The night so cold and still the lamp flame hardly
    moves.
Clouds condense and drench our stone walled hut.
Broken rushes clog the reed gate's way.
The stream gurgles, a torrent in its bed.
That's all we hear. Only rarely, comes a human voice...
But oh, how priceless is this peace of mind that fills us
As we sit on our heels and put on another Chan
    monk's robe!

— *Master Hsu Yun*

A martial arts student went to his teacher and said earnestly, "I am devoted to studying your martial system. How long will it take me to master it." The teacher's reply was casual, "Ten years." Impatiently, the student answered, "But I want to master it faster than that. I will work very hard. I will practice everyday, ten or more hours a day if I have to. How long will it take then?" The teacher thought for a moment, "20 years."

The Partial within the True:
The blue sky clears and the River of Stars' cold flood
    dries up.
At midnight the wooden boy pounds on the moon's
    door.
In darkness the jade woman is startled from her sleep.

The True within the Partial:
Ocean and clouds rendezvous at the top of the spirit
    mountain.
The old woman returns with hair hanging down like
    white silk
And shyly faces the mirror coldly reflecting her image.

— *Hongzhi*

The flower invites the butterfly with no-mind;
The butterfly visits the flower with no-mind.
The flower opens, the butterfly comes;
The butterfly comes, the flower opens.
I don't know others,
Others don't know me.
By not-knowing we follow nature's course.

— *Ryokan*

Nature has a perfect sense of composition that always seems to reflect perfect order.

We do not learn by experience, but by our capacity for experience.

I do not cut my life up into days but my days into lives, each day, each hour, an entire life.

This is this,
That is that,
Everything as it is:
A pine tree is green,
A flower is red.

You may try to be round,
But keep one corner,
O mind,
Otherwise you'll
Slip and roll away.

In the scenery of spring,
nothing is better, nothing worse;
The flowering branches are
of themselves, some short, some long.

During the civil wars in feudal Japan, an invading army would quickly sweep into a town and take control. In one particular village, everyone fled just before the army arrived—everyone except the Zen master. Curious about this old fellow, the general went to the temple to see for himself what kind of man this master was. When he wasn't treated with the deference and submissiveness to which he was accustomed, the general burst into anger. "You fool," he shouted as he reached for his sword, "don't you realise you are standing before a man who could run you through without blinking an eye!" But despite the threat, the master seemed unmoved. "And do you realise," the master replied calmly, "that you are standing before a man who can be run through without blinking an eye?"

A monk asked Pa-ling: "Are the views of Zen masters the same or different from what is taught in the sutras?"
Pa-ling answered: "When a rooster is cold, it flies up into a tree; when a duck is cold, it dives under the water."

The road enters green mountains near evening's dark;
Beneath the white cherry trees, a Buddhist temple
Whose priest doesn't know what regret for spring's
    passing means—
Each stroke of his bell startles more blossoms into
    falling.

— Keijo Shurin

Too lazy to be ambitious,
I let the world take care of itself.
Ten days' worth of rice in my bag;
a bundle of twigs by the fireplace.
Why chatter about delusion and enlightenment?
Listening to the night rain on my roof,
I sit comfortably, with both legs stretched out.

— Ryokan

When the mind is like wood or stone, there is
nothing to be discriminated.

— Pai-chang Huai-hai

Getting rid of things and clinging to emptiness
Is an illness of the same kind;
It is just like throwing oneself into a fire
To avoid being drowned.

— *Yungchia*

We are what we think.
All that we are arises with our thoughts.
With our thoughts we make the world.
Speak or act with an impure mind
And trouble will follow you
As the wheel follows the ox that draws the cart.

— *Dhammapada*

I gained nothing at all from supreme enlightenment,
and for that very reason it is called supreme
enlightenment.

— *The Buddha*

Rest in natural great peace this exhausted mind,
Beaten helpless by karma and neurotic thoughts
Like the relentless fury of the pounding waves
In the infinite ocean of samsara.
Rest in natural great peace.

— *Nyoshul Khen Rinpoche*

The mind is very difficult to see,
Very delicate and subtle;
It moves and lands wherever it pleases.
The wise one should guard his mind,
For a guarded mind brings happiness.

— *Dhammapada*

To have some deep feeling about Buddhism is not the
  point;
we just do what we should do,
like eating supper and going to bed.
This is Buddhism!

— *Suzuki Roshi*

Consumed with anger,
The world is an ugly place.
Bathed in happiness,
The world is a wonderful place.
But, aha! the same world.

— *Unno*

Our mind is like
A puppet show:
When a devil
Pushes itself forward,
A Buddha will hide.

Contentment that derives from knowing when to be content is eternal contentment.

Do not entertain hopes for realisation, but practice all your life.

Everything
Changing
In this floating world.
One thing staying the same:
Death.

No dependence upon words and letters; direct pointing at the soul of man; seeing into one's nature and the attainment of Buddhahood.

— *Bodhidharma*

What peace it is
Going to the shrine with
Nothing to pray for!

Zen master: "Who binds you?"
The seeker of liberty: "No one binds me."
Zen master: "Then why seek liberation?"